FOOD LOVER

PASTA

RECIPES SELECTED BY MARIKA KUCEROVA

Trans
Atlantic
Press

All recipes serve four people, unless otherwise indicated.

For best results when cooking the recipes in this book, buy fresh ingredients and follow the instructions carefully. Make sure that everything is properly cooked through before serving, particularly any meat and shellfish, and note that as a general rule vulnerable groups such as the very young, elderly people, pregnant women, convalescents and anyone suffering from an illness should avoid dishes that contain raw or lightly cooked eggs.

For all recipes, quantities are given in standard U.S. cups and imperial measures, followed by the metric equivalent. Follow one set or the other, but not a mixture of both because conversions may not be exact. Standard spoon and cup measurements are level and are based on the following:

1 tsp. = 5 ml, 1 tbsp. = 15 ml, 1 cup = 250 ml / 8 fl oz.

Note that Australian standard tablespoons are 20 ml, so Australian readers should use 3 tsp. in place of 1 tbsp. when measuring small quantities.

The electric oven temperatures in this book are given for conventional ovens with top and bottom heat. When using a fan oven, the temperature should be decreased by about 20–40°F / 10–20°C – check the oven manufacturer's instruction book for further guidance. The cooking times given should be used as an approximate guideline only.

CONTENTS

TAGLIATELLE WITH WHITE BEANS AND TOMATOES

Ingredients

14 oz / 400 g green tagliatelle

1 can cannellini beans (about 14 oz / 400 g)

2 tbsp. finely chopped fresh mint leaves

3 tbsp. olive oil

1 tbsp. lemon juice

1 clove garlic, finely chopped

1 cup / 140 g cherry tomatoes, cut in half

1 tbsp. lemon zest

Salt & freshly milled pepper

A few mint leaves to garnish

Method
Prep and cook time: 25 min

1 Cook the tagliatelle in boiling, salted water according to the instructions on the packet until al dente. In the meantime, drain and rinse the beans.

2 Heat the oil in a skillet and sauté the beans, mint, lemon juice, garlic and tomatoes for about 3–4 minutes, stirring occasionally.

3 Drain the pasta and mix with the beans. Season to taste with lemon zest, salt and pepper, garnish with mint leaves and serve.

SPAGHETTI CARBONARA

Ingredients

2 slices (rashers) fatty (streaky) bacon

2 tbsp. oil

14 oz / 400 g spaghetti

3 eggs

3 tbsp. light cream (single cream)

Salt & freshly milled pepper

Generous 1 cup / 100 g freshly grated Parmesan cheese

Some chives, chopped

2 cloves garlic

Method

Prep and cook time: 25 min

1 Cut the bacon into thin strips. Fry the bacon gently in the oil in a large pan.

2 Meanwhile, cook the spaghetti in boiling, salted water according to the instructions on the packet until al dente.

3 Whisk the eggs and cream and season with salt and pepper. Stir in half of the Parmesan cheese and the chives.

4 Remove the crispy bacon slices from the pan and keep warm. Peel the garlic, finely chop and gently sauté in the bacon fat.

5 Drain the spaghetti well, then place immediately in the pan and toss in the bacon fat. Now take the pan off the heat. Pour in the egg–cream mixture and stir until the spaghetti is coated with the sauce. Mix in the bacon, season with freshly milled pepper, sprinkle the remaining Parmesan cheese over the top and serve.

SPAGHETTI WITH SALMON AND DILL

Ingredients

14 oz / 400 g spaghetti

11 oz / 300 g salmon fillet

Some dill weed (dill)

1¼ cups / 300 ml light (single) cream

Salt & freshly milled pepper

2 tsp. freshly grated lemon zest

Method

Prep and cook time: 25 min

1 Cook the spaghetti in boiling, salted water until al dente.

2 Cut the salmon into bite-size pieces. Finely chop the dill, reserving a few sprigs for garnish.

3 Bring the cream, salt, pepper and lemon zest to a boil and cook over a high heat for about 2–3 minutes. Reduce the heat, add the salmon pieces and simmer for another 2–3 minutes. Season to taste with salt and pepper.

4 Drain the spaghetti, then toss the spaghetti and the dill in the sauce and serve garnished with a few dill sprigs.

PASTA WITH MUSHROOMS AND BACON

Ingredients

3½ cups / 400 g trofie pasta

7 oz / 200 g lean bacon

2 cups / 150 g mushrooms

2 large tomatoes

1 onion

Scant 1 cup / 100 g finely grated Emmental or Cheddar cheese

Salt & freshly milled pepper

Method

Prep and cook time: 25 min

1 Cook the pasta in boiling, salted water according to the instructions on the packet until al dente.

2 Dice the bacon. Clean and chop the mushrooms. Drop the tomatoes into boiling water for a few seconds, refresh in cold water, then skin, quarter, deseed and chop. Peel and finely chop the onion.

3 Fry the bacon in a dry skillet, then add the onion and the mushroom and sauté for about 5 minutes. Now add the tomatoes and the drained pasta and toss.

4 Remove the skillet from the heat and season with salt and pepper. Fold in half the cheese. Sprinkle the remaining cheese over the top before serving.

CHEESE SOUP WITH MACARONI AND VEGETABLES

Ingredients

2¼ cups / 250 g macaroni

1 large carrot

5 oz / 150 g spinach

1 shallot

1 small zucchini (courgette)

10 oz / 300 g Cheddar cheese, plus a little to garnish

2 tbsp. butter

¾–1 cup / 200 ml cider

1¼ cups / 300 ml milk

1¼ cups / 300 g whipping cream

2 tbsp. olive oil

½ tsp. sugar

Salt & freshly milled pepper

1 pinch grated nutmeg

Method

Prep and cook time: 30 min

1 Cook the pasta in boiling, salted water according to the instructions on the packet until al dente.

2 Peel the carrot; cut into quarters lengthways, then slice. Wash the spinach, then drain. Peel and finely chop the shallot. Slice the zucchini (courgette) into thin slices. Grate the cheese.

3 Heat the butter in a saucepan and sauté the shallot until soft. Add the cider, milk, cream and cheese, heat and stir until the cheese has melted. Cover and keep warm.

4 Heat 1 tablespoon of olive oil in a skillet and sauté the carrots until soft. Season with salt and pepper and sprinkle sugar over the top. Heat the remaining tablespoon of oil in another skillet and fry the zucchini (courgette) slices. Add the spinach and sauté. Season with salt, pepper and nutmeg.

5 Purée the sauce until smooth and creamy. Add the macaroni, bring to a boil and check the seasoning. Ladle into deep bowls. Add the vegetables (spinach, zucchini, carrots) and serve garnished with freshly grated cheese.

GINGERED SPAGHETTI WITH SHRIMPS AND PEAS

Ingredients

1½ cups / 400 g shrimp (prawns)

2 tbsp. lemon juice

2 thin leeks

2 cloves garlic

1 walnut-size piece fresh root ginger

2 tbsp. olive oil

1¼ cups / 200 g frozen peas

Scant ½ cup / 100 ml fish broth (stock)

14 oz / 400 g spaghetti

Some cilantro (fresh coriander)

Method

Prep and cook time: 25 min

1 Place the shrimp (prawns) in bowl and drizzle lemon juice over the top.

2 Trim the leeks and finely slice. Peel the garlic and the ginger and finely chop.

3 Heat the oil in a skillet, then sauté the garlic followed by the ginger. Now add the peas and the leeks and sauté. Pour in the fish broth (stock), cover and simmer for about 5 minutes over a medium heat.

4 Cook the spaghetti in boiling, salted water until al dente, then drain.

5 Put a few cilantro (coriander) leaves aside and finely chop the rest.

6 Put the shrimp and the chopped cilantro into the sauce and simmer for a few minutes, until the shrimp are cooked. Toss the spaghetti in the sauce and serve immediately in warmed bowls. Garnish with the remaining cilantro sprigs.

LINGUINE WITH CREAMY CEP MUSHROOMS

Ingredients

14 fl oz / 400 ml vegetable broth (stock)

2 tbsp. / 10 g dried cep mushrooms

7 oz / 200 g fresh cep mushrooms

1 onion

2 cloves garlic

14 oz / 400 g linguine

2 tbsp. olive oil

Salt & freshly milled pepper

3 tbsp. crème fraîche

2 tbsp. chopped fresh parsley

Method

Prep and cook time: 40 min

1 Warm the vegetable broth (stock) and soak the dried cep mushrooms in the broth for about 20 minutes.

2 Slice the fresh cep mushrooms. Peel and finely chop the onion and the garlic.

3 Cook the linguine in boiling, salted water until al dente.

4 Fry the fresh mushrooms in hot oil over a high heat. Add the onions and garlic and sauté, then season with salt and pepper.

5 Pour the soaked mushrooms into a sieve and catch the liquid. If possible, strain the liquid through a filter to make it clear.

6 Rinse the soaked mushrooms, then add to the fried mushrooms in the skillet along with the strained liquid. Bring to a boil and simmer for 3 minutes.

7 Stir in the crème fraîche and the chopped parsley. Season to taste with salt and pepper. Drain the linguine and serve with the creamy cep mushroom sauce.

SPINACH CANNELLONI

Ingredients

9 oz / 250 g cannelloni tubes (no pre-cook type)

1–2 tbsp. / 15–25g butter

For the filling:

1¼ lb / 500 g spinach

Scant 1 cup / 200 g ricotta cheese

1 egg

Salt & freshly milled pepper

Grated nutmeg

For the tomatoes:

7 oz / 200 g tomatoes

1 shallot

1 clove garlic

1 tbsp. olive oil

For the Béchamel sauce:

1 tbsp. / 15 g butter

1 tbsp. flour

1 cup / 250 ml milk

Salt & freshly milled pepper

1 cup / 75 g freshly grated Parmesan cheese

Method

Prep and cook time: 1 h

1 Preheat oven (400°F / 200°C / Gas Mark 6).

2 Wash the spinach well, put into a pan dripping wet and heat over a medium heat until it wilts. Drain, refresh in cold water, drain again and squeeze out.

3 Roughly chop the spinach and mix with the mashed ricotta cheese. Stir in the egg and season with salt, pepper and nutmeg.

4 Spoon the mixture into the cannelloni tubes and place them side by side in a greased baking dish.

5 Drop the tomatoes into boiling water for a few seconds, refresh in cold water, then skin, quarter, deseed and chop roughly.

6 Peel and finely chop the shallot and garlic. Heat the oil and sauté the shallot and garlic. Add the tomatoes and cook over a medium heat for about 5 minutes.

7 For the Béchamel sauce, melt the butter, stir in the flour and cook for a couple of minutes without browning. Then gradually stir in the milk. Simmer for 10 minutes, season with salt and pepper and stir in half of the Parmesan.

8 Spread the tomatoes on the cannelloni. Pour the Bechamel sauce over and sprinkle with the rest of the Parmesan cheese. Dot with butter and bake in the preheated oven for about 30 minutes.

PAPPARDELLE WITH WHITE BEANS AND TUNA

Ingredients

14 oz / 400 g pappardelle

5 oz / 140 g canned tuna

1 onion

2 cloves garlic

Scant 2 cups / 250 g canned cannellini beans

2 tbsp. olive oil

9oz / 250 g canned chopped tomatoes

Salt & freshly milled pepper

Chili flakes

A few small sage leaves, to garnish

Method

Prep and cook time: 30 min

1 Cook the pappardelle in boiling, salted water according to the package instructions until al dente.

2 Drain the tuna and break into small chunks. Peel and chop the onion and the garlic. Rinse the beans, then drain.

3 Heat the oil in a saucepan. Fry the onions and the garlic, stirring continually. Add the tomatoes and the beans, then season with salt, pepper and chili flakes. Simmer for about 10 minutes, then add the tuna and season to taste.

4 Drain the pasta, adding a few tablespoonfuls of the pasta water to the sauce. Toss the pasta in the sauce, then arrange in pre-warmed bowls and serve. Garnish with sage.

LINGUINE WITH CLAMS AND BASIL

Ingredients

1 lb 2 oz / 500 g linguine

2½ cups / 400 g cherry tomatoes

1 clove garlic, finely chopped

Scant ½ cup / 100 ml white wine

14 oz / 400 g clams, scrubbed and ready to cook

1 bunch basil

3 tbsp. olive oil

²/₃ cup / 50 g Parmesan cheese

Salt & freshly milled pepper

Method

Prep and cook time: 25 min

1 Cook the linguine in boiling, salted water according to the instructions, until al dente. Reserve some of the cooking water when draining.

2 Put the tomatoes into a pan with the chopped garlic. Add the white wine, cover and bring to a boil. Add the clams, cover and simmer over a low heat for about 5 minutes, until the clams have opened. Discard any clams that do not open.

3 Meanwhile purée the basil (reserving a few leaves for the garnish) with the olive oil, Parmesan cheese and a little of the pasta cooking water to make pesto.

4 Add the drained pasta to the clams and tomatoes and mix carefully. Stir in the pesto and season to taste with salt and pepper. Serve garnished with basil.

TAGLIATELLE WITH CHILI AND LEMON ZEST

Ingredients

1–2 unwaxed lemons

1 lb 2 oz / 500 g tagliatelle

4 red chilies

2 oz / 50 g spinach leaves or arugula (rocket)

1 tbsp. / 15 g butter

3–4 tbsp. olive oil

Salt & freshly milled pepper

Method

Prep and cook time: 25 min

1 Wash the lemons in hot water, then dry and grate the lemon zest. Cut one lemon in half and squeeze out the juice.

2 Cook the tagliatelle in boiling, salted water until al dente.

3 In the meantime, deseed and finely chop the chilies. Wash the spinach, then leave to drain.

4 Melt the butter in a skillet, sauté the lemon zest, then add the chilies and the olive oil. Season to taste with salt and lemon juice.

5 Drain the tagliatelle, then toss immediately in the lemon–butter sauce. Mix in the arugula leaves and serve on warmed plates. Sprinkle a little freshly milled pepper over the top before serving.

PENNE WITH SHRIMPS AND OLIVES

Ingredient

1 small onion

2 cloves garlic

6 ripe tomatoes

olive oil

2 tbsp. capers

4 tbsp. black olives, pitted

11 oz / 300 g raw shrimp (prawns), washed, peeled, de-veined

Salt & freshly milled pepper

1 tsp. sugar

4½ cups / 500 g penne

4 tbsp. chopped fresh parsley

Method

Prep and cook time: 25 min

1 Peel and finely chop the onion and the garlic. Chop the tomatoes. Rinse the capers in cold water, then drain.

2 Heat 3 tablespoons of olive oil in a skillet and sauté the onions and the garlic until soft. Add the tomatoes and a scant ½ cup / 100 ml of water, cover and simmer for 4–5 minutes over a medium heat.

3 Add the capers and the olives and simmer for a further 1 minute. Season to taste with salt, pepper and sugar. Now add the shrimps (prawns) and gently simmer over a low heat until cooked.

4 In the meantime cook the pasta in boiling, salted water until al dente. Drain the pasta, then toss in the sauce, together with the chopped parsley and 1–2 tablespoons of olive oil. Season to taste with salt and pepper and serve immediately.

PASTA WITH LEEK, BACON AND HERBS

Ingredients

4½ cups / 500 g farfalle

4 slices (rashers) bacon

1 leek

2 cloves garlic

2 tbsp. / 25 g butter

Scant ¾ cup / 60 g Parmesan cheese

Freshly milled pepper

Basil, shredded

Method

Prep and cook time: 30 min

1 Cook the pasta in plenty of boiling, salted water until al dente.

2 Cut the bacon into thin strips. Trim and wash the leek and cut the white and light green parts into thin rings. Peel the garlic. Heat the butter in a pan, add the bacon and fry briefly. Add the leek rings and press the garlic into the pan. Sauté briefly.

3 Mix the drained pasta with the bacon and leeks. Season with pepper. Serve sprinkled with Parmesan cheese shavings and shredded basil.

RIGATONI WITH CHICKEN AND BROCCOLI

Ingredients

4½ cups / 400 g rigatoni or tortiglioni

14 oz / 400 g grilled chicken

14oz / 400 g broccoli florets

1½ oz / 40 g sun-dried tomatoes

2 cloves garlic

4 tsp. oil

Salt & freshly milled pepper

1 lemon

2 tbsp. black olives, chopped

2–3 tbsp. chopped parsley

Method

Prep and cook time: 30 min

1 Cook the pasta in plenty of boiling, salted water until al dente.

2 Meanwhile, remove the chicken meat from the bones and cut into pieces.

3 Blanch the broccoli in boiling, salted water for 3–4 minutes, then refresh in cold water and drain.

4 Chop the sun-dried tomatoes. Peel and crush the garlic.

5 Heat the oil in a skillet and add the garlic, tomatoes and chicken. Season lightly with salt and pepper. Grate a little lemon zest into the pan, squeeze in the lemon juice and warm over a low heat for 8–10 minutes.

6 Add the broccoli and heat very gently for a further 5 minutes or so. Mix in the chopped olives and parsley and reheat.

7 Season to taste with salt and pepper. Then mix the sauce with the drained pasta and serve hot.

PENNE WITH PEPPERS, BACON AND MUSHROOMS

Ingredients

1 slice (rasher) bacon

1 onion

2 cloves garlic

1 red bell pepper

4 large mushrooms

2 tbsp. oil

11 oz / 300 g peeled tomatoes, canned

Salt & freshly milled pepper

3½ cups / 400 g penne

Freshly grated Parmesan cheese, to serve

Some basil leaves

Method

Prep and cook time: 40 min

1 Dice the bacon and fry in a dry skillet until crisp. Remove from the skillet and place on the side.

2 Peel and finely chop the garlic and the onion. Cut the bell peppers in half lengthways, de-seed, then slice into fine strips. Slice the mushrooms.

3 Heat the oil in a saucepan. Sauté the onion, garlic and strips of pepper. Add the drained tomatoes and season with salt and pepper. Cover with a lid and simmer gently for 15 minutes. Add the mushrooms about 5 minutes before the end of the cooking time.

4 Now stir in the bacon and season to taste with salt and pepper.

5 Cook the pasta in boiling, salted water according to the instructions on the packet until al dente. Drain, then toss in the sauce. Serve with a little grated Parmesan cheese and garnish with a few basil leaves.

SPICY SPAGHETTI WITH COD FILLET

Ingredients

4 cod fillets, each weighing about 4 oz / 125 g

2 tbsp. lime juice

1 red bell pepper

2 red chilis

1 clove garlic

14 oz / 400 g spaghetti

4 tbsp. olive oil

1–2 tbsp. tomato concentrate or passata

4 tbsp. vegetable broth (stock)

2 tbsp. freshly grated Parmesan cheese

1 tbsp. / 15 g butter

Salt & ground white pepper

Method

Prep and cook time: 30 min

1 Drizzle the fish with 1 tablespoon of lime juice. De-seed the chilies and slice into fine rings. Slice the bell pepper. Peel the garlic and finely chop.

2 Cook the spaghetti in boiling, salted water until al dente.

3 In the meantime, sauté the chili, garlic and bell pepper in hot oil. Add the tomato concentrate, then pour in the vegetable broth (stock) and the remaining lime juice. Fold in the Parmesan cheese and season to taste with salt and pepper.

4 Drain the spaghetti and toss with the sauce.

5 Fry the fish in butter on both sides until golden brown, season with salt, place on the spaghetti and serve.

SALMON LASAGNA WITH SPINACH AND PARMESAN

Ingredients

Approx. 12 lasagna sheets (cooked according to package instructions)

1 lb 4 oz / 600 g salmon

4 handfuls spinach

1 clove garlic

4 tbsp. / 50 g butter

4 tbsp. flour

3 cups / 750 ml milk

4 tbsp. crème fraîche

Salt & freshly milled pepper

Grated nutmeg

6 sprigs thyme

4 tbsp. freshly grated Parmesan cheese

2 tbsp. butter

Method

Prep and cook time: 1 h 20 min

1 Heat the oven to 350°F (180°C / Gas Mark 4).

2 Cut the salmon into slices approximately ¾ inch (2 cm) thick. Wash the spinach. Peel and finely chop the garlic.

3 Melt half the butter in a pan and gradually stir in the flour. Cook gently for 2 minutes, stirring all the time, then gradually stir in the milk. Add the creme fraiche, season with salt and pepper and simmer for 10 minutes.

4 Melt the remaining butter in a clean pan and gently cook the garlic until soft but not brown. Add the spinach with 2 tablespoons of water, put a lid on the pan and cook for 3-4 minutes or until the spinach has wilted then season with salt, pepper and the nutmeg.

5 Drain the spinach and roughly chop.

6 Put a small amount of the white sauce on the bottom of an ovenproof dish, then layer the lasagne, salmon, white sauce and spinach, finishing with a layer of sauce.

7 Scatter over the Parmesan cheese then bake in the oven for 35–45 minutes. Serve garnished with thyme.

PASTA SALAD
WITH ANCHOVIES, CAPERS, OLIVES AND PARMESAN

Ingredients

4½ cups / 500 g casarecce, or other medium-size pasta

15 anchovies (in oil)

20 cherry tomatoes

1 handful fresh basil

30 black olives

6–7 tbsp. capers, drained

⅔ cup / 50 g freshly grated Parmesan cheese, to garnish

Dressing:

2 cloves garlic

4–5 tbsp. balsamic vinegar

6–7 tbsp. olive oil

1 pinch sugar

Salt & white pepper

Method
Prep and cook time: 45 min

1 Cook the pasta in plenty of boiling, salted water until al dente, then drain, refresh in cold water and drain thoroughly. Put into a bowl.

2 Halve the anchovies and add to the pasta.

3 Quarter the tomatoes. Mix all the salad ingredients with the pasta, reserving a few basil leaves to garnish.

4 For the dressing, peel, halve and finely chop the garlic. Whisk together the vinegar, oil, sugar and garlic and season well with salt and pepper. Pour the dressing over the pasta salad and mix well. Let stand for about 30 minutes.

5 Then check the seasoning and garnish the salad with a few Parmesan shavings and basil leaves.

PENNE WITH PEAS AND GREEN BEANS

Ingredients

9 oz / 250 g green beans

3½ cups / 400 g penne

1 clove garlic

3–4 tbsp. olive oil

2¼ cups / 250 g frozen peas

1–2 tbsp. finely chopped mixed herbs, such as basil, parsley, mint

²/₃ cup / 50 g freshly grated Parmesan cheese

Salt & freshly milled pepper

Method

Prep and cook time: 30 min

1 Trim the green beans and blanch in boiling, salted water until al dente. Drain, refresh in cold water, then leave to drain. Cut the beans into 1 inch (2–3 cm) pieces.

2 Cook the penne in boiling, salted water until al dente.

3 In the meantime, peel and finely chop the garlic. Fry the garlic in hot oil, then add the peas and sauté. Now stir in the beans and sauté. Add the chopped herbs and the Parmesan cheese and season to taste with salt and pepper.

4 Drain the pasta, toss with the vegetables and serve immediately.

MANICOTTI WITH TOMATO SAUCE AND CHEESE

Ingredients

1 lb 2 oz / 500 g manicotti (or cannelloni)

Scant 1 cup / 100 g grated cheese (e.g. Emmental)

Basil, to garnish

Butter, for the dish

For the tomato sauce:

3 tbsp. extra virgin olive oil

1 large onion, diced

1 can chopped tomatoes (about 14 oz / 400 g)

3 cloves garlic, peeled

Sugar

Salt & freshly milled pepper

Grated nutmeg

For the meat–cheese sauce:

1 tbsp. /15 g clarified butter or oil

1¾ cups/ 400 g ground (minced) meat

1 onion, finely chopped

1 clove garlic

2 small carrots, peeled and finely diced

½ fennel bulb, trimmed and finely diced

1 bay leaf

1 tbsp. flour

¼ cup / 50 ml dry white wine

Scant 1 cup / 200 ml vegetable broth (stock)

Scant ½ cup / 100 ml whipping cream

Grated nutmeg

Scant 1¼ cups / 100 g freshly grated Parmesan cheese

Salt & freshly milled pepper

Method

Prep and cook time: 1 h 40 min

1 For the tomato sauce, heat the oil in a deep skillet and sauté the onion until translucent. Add the tomatoes. Then reduce the heat, press the garlic into the sauce, cover and simmer over a low heat for 25 minutes.

2 Add 1 teaspoon of sugar and season well with salt, pepper and freshly grated nutmeg. Cover and simmer for a further 10 minutes, then purée the sauce.

3 For the meat–cheese sauce, heat the clarified butter and fry the ground meat, breaking it up

to brown right through. Add the vegetables and bay leaf and fry for a few minutes. Season with salt and pepper and dust with flour, then add the wine, broth (stock) and cream and simmer for 10-15 minutes to produce a thick sauce. Remove the bay leaf, add nutmeg to taste and stir in the grated Parmesan cheese.

4 Preheat the oven to 400°F (200°C /Gas Mark 6). Butter a baking dish. Fill the manicotti with meat sauce and lay in the baking dish. Pour the tomato sauce over, sprinkle with grated cheese and bake in the preheated oven (middle shelf) for about 40 minutes.

PENNE WITH SPICY TUNA

Ingredients

14 oz / 400 g tuna fillet

2 tbsp. lime juice

1 red onion

2 cloves garlic

7oz / 200 g canned tomatoes

½ cup / 50 g black olives, pitted

2 red chilies

3½ cups / 400 g penne

4 tbsp. olive oil

3–4 tbsp. capers

Salt

Tabasco sauce

Method

Prep and cook time: 40 min

1 Cut the tuna fillet into pieces and drizzle lime juice over the top.

2 Peel and finely chop the onion and the garlic. Drain the tomatoes and chop, retaining the tomato juice. Slice the olives. Finely chop the chilies.

3 Cook the penne in boiling, salted water until al dente.

4 Fry the onion and the garlic in hot oil, then add the tuna, followed by the tomatoes and the tomato juice. Now add the chilies, olives and capers and season with salt. Simmer the sauce until the liquid has reduced a little, then season to taste with the Tabasco sauce.

5 Drain the pasta and toss in the tuna sauce. Serve in warmed bowls.

SPAGHETTI WITH SUN-DRIED TOMATOES

Ingredients

14 oz / 400 g spaghetti

5 oz / 150 g sun-dried tomatoes

2 cloves garlic

4 tbsp. olive oil

4 tbsp. ground almonds

1 pinch sugar

Sea salt & freshly milled pepper

Juice and zest of 1 lemon

2/3 cup / 50 g freshly grated Parmesan cheese

1 handful basil leaves, to garnish

Method

Prep and cook time: 30 min

1 Cook the spaghetti in boiling, salted water until al dente.

2 Roughly chop the dried tomatoes. Peel and finely chop the garlic.

3 Heat the olive oil in a large pan and gently fry the garlic until soft but not brown.

4 Add the tomatoes, cook for 3 minutes, stirring all the time, then stir in the almonds, season with the sugar, salt and pepper and continue cooking for 2 more minutes.

5 When the spaghetti is cooked, drain well then return to the pan with the tomato mixture and lemon juice and zest. Mix well. Serve in warmed bowls scattered with the Parmesan cheese and garnished with the basil.

Published by Transatlantic Press

First published in 2010

Transatlantic Press
38 Copthorne Road, Croxley Green, Hertfordshire WD3 4AQ

© Transatlantic Press

Images and Recipes by StockFood © The Food Image Agency

Recipes selected by Marika Kucerova, StockFood

A catalogue record for this book is available from the British Library.

ISBN 978-1-908533-46-3

Printed in China